This book is sold on the understanding that the publisher and author are not engaged in providing medical, legal or other professional advice or services. The information provided within is for your general knowledge only. If you require professional or medical advice or treatment for a specific condition, the services of a competent, qualified professional person should be sought promptly. Achieving and maintaining a healthy weight is an ambition that would benefit most overweight adults and following a diet plan can help achieve this. However, the 5:2 diet plan is not suitable for:

- anyone who is pregnant, planning a pregnancy or breast-feeding
- anyone with a major health condition such as diabetes, irritable bowel syndrome
- anyone who has had an eating disorder.

In any case, you should consult your doctor before commencing a new diet or exercise regime.

This book is designed to provide general information in regard to the subject matter. While reasonable attempts have been made to verify the accuracy of the information provided, neither the author nor the publisher assumes any responsibility for errors, omissions, interpretations or usage of the subject matters within.

Warning on Allergic reactions – some recipes included in this book use nuts or nut oils. These specific recipes should be avoided by:

- anyone with a known nut allergy
- anyone who may be vulnerable to nut allergies such as pregnant and nursing mothers, invalids, the elderly, babies and children.

Warning on Eggs – The UK Department of Health's advice is that eggs should not be consumed raw. Some recipes included in this book are made with raw or lightly cooked eggs. These specific recipes should be avoided by:

- anyone who may be vulnerable such as pregnant and nursing mothers, invalids, the elderly, babies and children.

Contents

Introduction

Background to The Two-Day 5:2 Diet Plan

If you are reading this book, then it is probably fair for me to assume that you are interested in eating low calorie recipes cooked in a slow cooker. You may also be very familiar with the concept of the 5:2 Diet regime. Alternatively, perhaps you've just heard about this latest "wonder diet" and you're curious to find out to what it's all about? The 5:2 Diet is a diet regime based on the principle of Intermittent Fasting, whereby you choose to "fast" from food for certain periods of time.

However, don't panic, whilst Intermittent Fasting has been practised in some cultures and religions for centuries, the form it takes in the 5:2 Diet doesn't involve true fasting, rather it refers to a significantly reduced calorie-intake over short periods (more below). Over the last few years, the 5:2 Diet has become one of the most popular and widely followed weight-loss regimes. Its rise in popularity as a weight-loss regime was sparked by a BBC television documentary, first broadcast in 2012, which examined the weight-loss and health benefits that could be gained from following what the programme dubbed 'The 5:2 Diet'.

What is the Two-Day 5:2 Diet Plan & Why is it so Popular?

In a nutshell, on the 5:2 Diet you just diet on 2 days a week and then eat normally (but healthily) on the remaining 5 days. It is this simple and extremely easy to follow concept which is the first reason why this diet has become so popular.

This means that it is a very convenient diet plan to follow even if you normally struggle to incorporate dieting into your lifestyle, perhaps because you work shifts, or travel on business, for example.

The 5:2 Diet also suits anyone who has struggled to maintain their will-power or become very bored of the routine when dieting over a sustained period of time. With the 5:2 Diet Plan, as you diet for just two (non-consecutive) days a week, you:

- only need to maintain will-power in short bursts
- don't get bored as within 24 hrs you can eat whatever tickles your taste buds!

How Does the Two-Day 5:2 Diet Plan Lead to Weight Loss?

The 5:2 diet plan **works as your weekly calorie intake is in deficit** compared to what your body needs to maintain your current weight when you combine:

eating normally but healthily for 5 days + 2 days of restricted calorie intake.

This weekly calorie deficit leads to weight-loss, as long as you **don't treat it as a license to binge on the non-diet days**. What's more, once you have lost weight, you can really **easily maintain that loss** by moving onto a 6:1 regime, meaning that instead of dieting for 2 days a week, you reduce this to just 1 day a week.

Technically, your fast-diet-day calorie allowance should be a quarter of your recommended daily calorie intake. This does vary dependent upon your current weight and level of activity. However, part of the joy of the 5:2 diet plan is its simplicity, and there is a short-cut for this calculation. Most people following the 5:2 diet adopt the plan of sticking to a diet-day allowance of:

- 500 calories for women
- 600 calories for men.

A scientific study published in 2010 (Int J Obes (Lond)) found the Two-Day 5:2 Diet to be as effective at losing weight and improving insulin sensitivity as following a daily calorie-controlled diet. You can reasonably expect that the weekly calorie deficit created by following the Tow-Day 5:2 diet as described above to lead to a **weight loss of 1-2lbs per week**.

Is the Two-Day 5:2 Diet Plan Healthy and is it Suitable for Everyone?

There have been a number of scientific studies that have reported that there are wider health benefits to be gained from a healthy eating plan that incorporates intermittent fasting. Studies have found a correlation between intermittent fasting and lowered blood pressure, lowered cholesterol levels and improvements in insulin sensitivity (Nutrition & Metabolism 2012, Proceedings of the Nutrition Society 2012).

That said you should consult your doctor before commencing a new diet or exercise regime and that includes this plan. In particular, fasting is not suitable for everyone so the 5:2 diet plan **is not suitable for** some people, and particularly it is not appropriate for:

- anyone who is pregnant, planning a pregnancy or breast-feeding
- anyone with a major health condition such as diabetes, irritable bowel syndrome
- anyone who has had an eating disorder.

The Two-Day 5:2 Diet Plan

Diet for Two Days, Feast for Five!

The Easy Three Steps to the Two-Day 5:2 Diet Plan

The plan is so straightforward that it can be explained in just three simple steps, here's what you need to do:

1. At the start of the week, decide which two days are going to be your diet days in that week. A "diet day" is 24 hours long and can start at any point in the day to suit your schedule. You don't need to stick to the same days every week.

2. On your diet day, you must only eat 500 calories (for women) or 600 calories (for men). This needs to cover *everything you eat and drink* in that 24 hour period.

3. On the other five days, ***dine normally and mainly healthily*** (but treats are allowed)! Just remember that the two diet days are there to create a weekly calorie shortfall which leads to weight-loss, so just make sure you **don't overeat on the non-diet days**.

What is the "16 Hour Rule" on the Two-Day 5:2 Diet Plan?

The simple premise of the 5:2 diet is that, twice a week, you just eat 500 or 600 calories within a 24 hr period. Perhaps you have also **heard about a "16 hour rule"** and wondered what this is? The "16 hour rule" refers to the period of time between the last food eaten on your non-fasting day to the first food eaten on your fast day. Some of the research on the health benefits that can be gained from following a fasting diet regime found that there was a link from extending the period of time of fasting (ie no food consumption at all), especially to a period of 16 hours.

What does this mean in reality? Let's assume that on the day before you fast, you finished eating your evening meal at 7pm and that is the last food you eat that day. Following the "16 hour rule" in this example would mean that you wouldn't eat again on your fast day until 11am ie 16 hrs after 7pm.

Not everyone on the 5:2 diet follows the "16 hour rule", it is unlikely to make much (if any) difference to weight-loss, but it is associated with the wider health benefits related to following an intermittent diet regime.

Breakfast, Lunch and Dinner?

When you are on your fast-diet-day with calories restricted to 500/600 cals, you need to decide which meals you want to eat. For example, are you going to spread your calorie allowance over the 3 traditional meals of breakfast, lunch and dinner or will you skip a meal and therefore have more calories to spend on the remaining 2 meals?

If you decide to also follow the "16-hour rule", it probably makes sense to skip breakfast altogether and just have lunch and dinner.

However I know many people who feel that they **need to have breakfast** or they just don't have the energy to face the day. Ultimately, how many meals you eat on your fast-diet-days is a matter of personal choice for you, and there is no reason why you can't mix it up, eating 3 meals on some days and 2 on others. This book includes some suggested menu plans for both 500 and 600 calorie days with or without breakfast.

It is also important to carefully count calories on your fast-diet-days. If you just "guestimate" it is all to easy to blow your daily calories allowance, and sticking to 500/600 calories on your fast diet days is key to success on this programme.

Fortunately, this is where **this cookbook comes into play** – an array of tasty, filling, delicious but calorie-counted breakfasts, lunches and dinners – all designed to help you stick to your calorie plan on your fast days.

Have you previously been a Yo-Yo Dieter?

Are you are someone who has tried and failed to diet before, have you previously been a "yo-yo" dieter? By this I mean that you've started a diet with great intentions and the will-power of a saint, but after a period of time (and that may be a week, a month, 6 months), suddenly you've faltered and that falter has resulted in a binge. Often this is because a diet is about restrictions and forbidden items, and you need to keep to that regime day-in, day out, week-in, week-out. We are all human, and often we eat for reasons that are more than just to give us the energy we need to exist. We eat to celebrate and to commiserate, we eat out of boredom, we eat out of joy, we eat to be social and many more reasons besides.

If you have been through the cycle of yo-yo dieting previously, the 5:2 Diet is the antithesis of this. It could be argued that it would actually suit anyone who has "yo-yo"d in the past, as this behaviour shows that you do have the self-discipline to stick to a regime for a period of time, but with this diet, you only have to keep to the regime for a maximum of 24 hours at a time, and you're asleep for about 1/3rd of that time!

Successfully Using Your Slow Cooker or Crockpot on the Two-Day 5:2 Diet Plan

A slow cooker or crockpot has been one of the most popular, stand-alone kitchen appliances since the 1970s. With its slow, low heat cooking method, it is both economical and convenient. With our busy, modern lives, slow cooking is also a great way to prepare our meals on the 5:2 Diet Plan. On your diet days, you can do all your preparation in advance and then come home to the delicious aromas of a flavoursome and perfectly portioned meal, piping-hot and ready to be eaten straight away. How perfect! This goes a long way to helping avoid caving into temptation on your days, particularly if you have a long and hard journey home at the end of the day.

7 Top Tips For Successful Slow Cooking

1. **Size matters!** By this I mean that most of the recipes in this book lend themselves to being cooked in a smaller capacity slow cooker, such as a 2-3 litre (3½ - 5 pints) size model.
2. **Keep it Even.** As with all slow-cooker recipes, your ingredients should be cut into evenly sized pieces.
3. **Remove Fat.** When preparing meat for the slow cooker, all visible fat should be removed as should any skin.
4. ***Prep for Flavour**. Invest a little bit of time (10-15 mins max) in preparation! Now I know that this will be a little controversial to some, as there are many people who believe it is anathema to slow-cooking to use any sort of additional cooking pan as well or to do any sautéing/browning in advance of setting the slow-cooker to go. Despite this, I would just like to explain why I think that this extra step is worthwhile.*

   You will see that many of the recipes in this book call for some of the ingredients to be sautéed in advance of being added to the slow cooker. This step intensifies their flavours, the caramelisation adds depth and complexity to the dish, and it also improves the finished appearance. Many slow cookers now offer a sauté function to aid this process or they have pots that can be used directly on the stove top before being attached to the slow cooker mechanism.

However, if you disagree with me strongly on this, please do not worry, you can just skip this step in any recipe. The finished dish will be slightly less complex in flavour but it will still work. The choice is entirely yours.

5. **Know your own slow cooker**, guide times have been provided for each recipe but only you will know if your slow cooker cooks faster or slower in comparison.

6. **Prepare Ahead**. You can often prepare the ingredients in advance the evening before, then store in the fridge overnight in a sealable, airtight container and add to the slow cooker in the morning.

7. **Boil Beans**. Care must be taken with dried beans when cooking in a slow cooker. Make sure that the beans are soaked for at least 5 hrs in advance of use, then drain and rinse. Put into a saucepan with fresh cold water, bring to the boil and boil rapidly for 10 mins, drain and rinse before adding to the slow cooker, then cook thoroughly on low for 8 hrs. Make sure you add any salt to the dish at the end of cooking not the start.

7 More Tips & Hints for Two-Day 5:2 Diet Plan Fast-Day Dieting

1. Measure accurately - on your diet days, it is really important to measure precisely as this has a big impact on the accuracy of the calorie count of a dish. I recommend the following kitchen tools that really will help keep your calorie intake true on your diet-days:

   1.1 A standard set of measuring spoons: 1/8th tsp, ¼ tsp, ½ tsp, ½ tbsp, 1 tbsp

   1.2 If following the UK measures, a set of digital kitchen scales and a small measuring jug, OR,

   1.3 If following the American measures, then standard set of cup measures: ¼ cup, 1/3 cup, ½ cup, 1 cup

2. Taste matters - individual calorie counts have been included for each ingredient so that you can adjust a recipe to suit your taste or dietary preferences. However, don't be tempted to cut out some of the more calorie-dense ingredients such as Parmesan cheese just to "save" calories. The quantities used have been carefully worked out that they make *a big difference to the TASTE of the finished recipe* without compromising the overall calorie-count.

3. Track what you eat -on the days that you are dieting, make sure you tot-up all your calories and make a note of them. Write them down or track them on your mobile phone or tablet. As well as there not being much of a margin for error on fast days, tracking leads to conscious consumption.
4. Plan your fast days to suit your diary - whilst it can be helpful to have a routine and regular days in the week that are your "diet-days", your can be confident that you can change which days in a week you fast/diet on to suit your diary in that week.
5. Plan ahead -work out in advance what you are going to eat on your fast days, and buy the ingredients ahead of time. It's not a good plan to be wandering the oh-so-tempting aisles of the supermarket on your fast day, nor to get home after a hard day in the office and be faced with "what should I cook tonight".
6. Keep hydrated. It's an old adage that often we mistake thirst for hunger. Plus, proper hydration can help you feel fuller. You can drink water, tea, herb tea, coffee and calorie-free sodas or squashes. Aim to drink 8 good glasses per day (and not just on Diet Days).
7. Keep occupied. Make sure you have activities, errands and/or chores planned to occupy your mind on Diet Days. Boredom is also often mistaken for hunger, so keep your mind and fingers busy!

Eating Well on your 5 Non-Diet Days

As stated previously, the 5:2 diet is not a license to binge or overeat on your 5 non-diet days. On these days, you will eat normally but healthily. However, what does this actually mean? A healthy balanced diet means eating meals rich in fruit, vegetables, wholegrain cereals and one that is low in saturated fat and salt. However, this doesn’t mean foods lacking in taste, flavour or interest – quite the opposite! So, on your non-diet days try to follow this general approach:

eat more:

- fruit and vegetables
- wholegrain breads and cereals,
- pulses (peas, beans and lentils)
- nuts and seeds
- fish, both white and oily varieties

and less:

- high saturated fat dairy
- red meat

Buy the best quality ingredients that you can afford. I always use free range eggs (luckily, I am able to buy mine from the lovely 'Chicken Lady' across the road so they are as fresh as can be and from very happy chickens), I make sure that the meat I eat is from animals that have been well-cared for and that fish is sustainably-sourced. Whilst these ingredients are a little more expensive, I balance this because my recipes include plenty of inexpensive pulses, fruit and vegetables.

To keep the calorie levels very low on the 2 fast-diet days, the recipes for these days are generally very, very low in both total and saturated fat, as fat is very calorie-dense (1g = 9 calories or 1 teaspoon = 45 calories). Whilst it is essential for good health to not regularly eat a lot of saturated fat, it is important to include "good" fats in your diet ie unsaturated fats. These can be found in oily fish, avocado and oils sourced from corn, rapeseed, olives, sunflower seeds and other vegetable, nut and seed oils. They are also present in the vegetable spreads made from those oils. Try to make sure you include some of these great tasting foods in your meals on your non-diet days.

If you are looking for inspiration on cooking normally but healthily on your non-diet days, then you may be interested in my cookbook - **Mediterranean Diet Recipe Cookbook 100+ Heart Healthy Recipes**, available as both a paperback and ebook.

How to Use this Recipe Cookbook

Metric vs American Measurements

All recipes are provided in both Metric and American measurements. In order to provide meaningful equivalents, there may be slight "rounding" differences between the two systems, but these do not make a material difference to the overall calorie count. Egg sizes differ between Europe and the US. All recipes in this book are based on European Medium Eggs which is equivalent to American Large Eggs. Please do not mix Metric and American measurements, especially for baking recipes.

Both European English and American English names have been given for ingredients where they differ in common usage, for example, Fresh Coriander or Fresh Cilantro.

Standard **level** spoon measurements are used in all recipes

- 1 tsp = 5ml
- 1 tbsp = 15ml
- A pinch = 1/8 tsp

Individual Ingredient Calorie Counts

The calorie count for individual ingredients has been included in every recipe, which allows the reader to easily adapt the recipe if they do not like or cannot source a specific ingredient. This has been calculated on the metric weight. Additionally, when allocating calories to individual ingredients often there is a need to round up or down, each recipe adds up to its correct recipe total, but there may be slight rounding differences on the calories of an individual ingredient. Again, this does not make a material difference to the overall calorie count.

Cooking for 1 or 2?

This cookbook provides a variety of recipes whether you are cooking for one, two or more. In addition, wherever appropriate, recommendations are made for how to freeze or store the additional portions for future consumption.

Vegetarian Recipes & Vegetarian Options

Recipes suitable for Vegetarians are indicated with the V symbol. In addition, wherever possible in non-vegetarian recipes, alternative vegetarian options have been given on how to adapt the recipe to make it suitable for Vegetarians. Where a recipe includes cheese but is indicated with a V symbol, it assumes that the cook will use vegetarian cheese if that is required.

500 CALORIE EXAMPLE MENU PLANS

DAILY MENUS WITH BREAKFAST, LUNCH & DINNER

Example 1: Total Calories In Menu = 484

Breakfast: *Slow-Cooker Breakfast Fruit Compote*

Lunch: *London Particular Soup*

Dinner: *Slow Cooker Chicken Chile Blanco*

Example 2: Total Calories In Menu = 483

Breakfast: *Raspberry, Peach & Apricot Parfaits*

Lunch: *Autumn Harvest Festival Soup*

Dinner: *Coconut Prawn & Spinach Dahl with steamed brown basmati rice*

Example 3: Total Calories In Menu = 497

Breakfast: *Breakfast Baked Apples*

Lunch: *Tuscan Bean & Rosemary Soup*

Dinner: *Slow Roast Turkey Breast with Boulangère Potatoes*

DAILY MENUS WITH LUNCH & DINNER

Example 1: Total Calories In Menu = 467

Lunch: *Cauliflower & Stilton Soup with 2x SCracked Black Pepper Croutons*

Dinner: *Slow Cooker Meatballs with Wholewheat Spaghetti*

Example 2: Total Calories In Menu = 468

Lunch: *Creamy Fish Chowder with Garlic & Rosemary Croutons*

Dinner: *Chicken Palaver*

Example 3: Total Calories In Menu = 461

Lunch: *Lentil & Sweet Potato Soup with Tomato & Basil Croutons*

Dinner: *BBQ Chicken with Spicy Potato Wedges*

600 CALORIE EXAMPLE MENU PLANS

DAILY MENUS WITH BREAKFAST, LUNCH & DINNER

Example 1: Total Calories In Menu = 566

Breakfast: *Slow-Cooker Boston Baked Beans*

Lunch: *Minted Pea & Leek Soup with 2x Sea Salt & Cracked Black Pepper Croutons*

Dinner: *Aromatic Duck Pilaf*

Example 2: Total Calories In Menu = 591

Breakfast: *Coddled Eggs with Soldiers*

Lunch: *Mexican Chicken Soup*

Dinner: *Beef in Guinness Stew*

Example 3: Total Calories In Menu = 585

Breakfast: *Raspberry, Peach & Apricot Parfaits*

Lunch: *Ribollita Soup*

Dinner: *Slow Cooker Pork & Pepper Chilli Pot with steamed brown basmati rice*

DAILY MENUS WITH LUNCH & DINNER

Example 1: Total Calories In Menu = 577

Lunch: *Sun-dried Tomato Humous with Vegetable Crudités*

Dinner: *2 x Stuffed Peppers*

Example 2: Total Calories In Menu = 587

Lunch: *Lentil & Sweet Potato Soup with 2x Tomato & Basil Croutons*

Dinner: *Chickpea, Spinach & Mushroom Goan Curry & basmati rice, Baked Apple*

Example 3: Total Calories In Menu = 540

Lunch: *Cauliflower & Stilton Soup with 2x Garlic & Rosemary Croutons*

Dinner: *Slow Roast Turkey Breast with Boulangère Potatoes, Raspberry, Peach & Apricot Parfaits*

BREAKFASTS 150 CALS & UNDER

BREAKFAST FRUIT COMPOTE (V)

Ingredients with cals per serving

- ½ vanilla pod
- 1 cinnamon stick
- pinch freshly ground nutmeg
- 265g (9½ oz) firm pears c2 – 31 cals
- 75g (2½ oz) ripe plums c2 – 7 cals
- 28g (1 oz) ready-to-eat dried apricots c4 – 13 cals
- 28g (1 oz) dried figs c2 – 16 cals
- 155g (5½ oz) orange c.1 – 17 cals
- 2½ tsp honey – 10 cals
- 8 tsp fat-free, natural fromage frais – 5 cals

Directions

Thinly pare 2 strips of zest from the orange and split the vanilla bean in half length-wise and scrape out the seeds with the back of the knife. Put the zest, vanilla seeds and vanilla pod into a slow-cooker or Crock-Pot along with the juice of the orange, the honey and spices.

Peel the pears and cut into quarters, remove the core and pop into the poaching liquid. Remove the stones from the plums and cut into quarters. Cut the dried apricots in half and the figs into quarters. Add all these fruits to the slow-cooker. Cover with the lid and cook on low for 2-3 hours, gently turning the fruits every hour, until the pears are tender. Add a splash of water if the fruits look too dry.

Allow to cool and transfer to an airtight, sealable container and store in the fridge until ready to serve. Only remove the spices when you are ready to serve as they will continue to flavour the fruits whilst they are cooling. Serve a quarter of the fruit compote with 2 tsp of fat-free natural fromage frais.

Cooking for 1 or 2? Prepare & Store Meal Tip: These poached fruits will keep for up to 5 days in a sealed container stored in the fridge.

Serves: 4	Ready In: 2-3 hrs	Per Serving: 100 Calories

Raspberry, Peach & Apricot Parfaits V

Ingredients with cals per serving

- 42g (1½ oz) ready to eat dried apricots c6 – 19 cals
- 280g (9¾ oz) firm ripe fresh peaches c2 – 25 cals
- 70g (½ cup) fresh raspberries – 6 cals
- 4 tsp maple syrup
- 1 vanilla bean pod
- 1 lemon – 5 cals
- 1 cinnamon stick
- 4 tsp porridge oats – 6 cals
- 1 tsp ground cinnamon – 2 cals
- 6 tbsp (90g) 0% Greek yogurt – 26 cals

Directions

Make the compote the evening before and store overnight in the fridge.

To peel the peaches, bring a pan of water to boil. Score a cross into the bottom of each peach, then add to the boiling water, blanch for 40 secs to 1 min. Remove with a slotted spoon. When cool enough to handle, slip off the skin, then cut in half and remove the stone. Cut each half into four segments. Cut the dried apricots in half.

Place the peaches and apricots into a slow-cooker or CrockPot, along with the zest and juice of the lemon, maple syrup and cinnamon stick. Split the vanilla pod in half length wise, scrape out the seeds and add these and the pod to the fruit. Cover with the lid and cook on low for 2-3 hours, gently turning the fruits every hour, until the peach slices are tender. Add a splash of water if the fruits look too dry whilst cooking.

When cooked, stir in the raspberries and transfer to an airtight, sealable container. Allow to cool, then seal and store in the fridge until ready to serve. Only remove the spices when you are ready to serve as they will continue to flavour the fruits whilst they are cooling.

Meanwhile, heat a non-stick sauté pan over a medium heat and toast the porridge oats. Keep tossing the oats, taking care not to burn them. When cooked, remove to a ramekin and stir in the ground cinnamon. Set aside until the morning, then divide the peach compote between 4 serving glasses, followed by half of the Greek yogurt and then repeat. Sprinkle the cinnamon oats over the top and serve.

Cooking for 1 or 2? Prepare & Store Meal Tip: These poached fruits and cinnamon oats will keep for up to 5 days in separate, sealed containers stored in the fridge.

Serves: 4 | Ready In: 2-3 hrs (plus 30 mins chilling time) | Per Serving: 101 Calories

Boston Baked Beans

Directions

Place the dried beans in a large saucepan with 0.5 gallons (2 litres) of cold water, bring it to the boil and boil rapidly for 10 minutes. Then remove from the heat and set aside for 50 minutes. Roughly chop the bacon rashers. Drain the partially cooked beans, reserving 2 cups (500ml) of the liquid. Put the beans and bacon into the slow cooker along with the reserved bean stock and all the other ingredients except the salt. Give everything a really good stir.

Put on the lid and set to cook on low for at least 6 hours or overnight. In the morning, check the beans for seasoning and moisture, remove the bay leaves, add a small pinch of salt and/or a splash of water if required. Add a dash or 2 of Tabasco Sauce if you like a little more spice.

Vegetarian Option: Omit the Bacon.

Ingredients with cals per serving

- 150g (¾ cup) dried cannellini beans – 84 cals
- 230g (1 scant cup) tinned chopped tomatoes – 14 cals
- 2 extra trimmed bacon rashers (eg Weight Watchers) – 18 cals
- 1½ tsp tomato purée – 2 cals
- 1 tbsp (apple) cider vinegar – 1 cals
- ½ tsp dry mustard powder – 2 cals
- 1 tbsp Worcestershire Sauce – 4 cals
- 2 tsp black treacle (molasses) – 7 cals
- 1 tbsp dark brown sugar – 15 cals
- ¼ tsp cayenne pepper
- 2 bay leaves
- pinch kosher/sea salt
- pinch ground black pepper

Cooking for 1 or 2? Prepare & Freeze Meal Tip: Divide the cooked Baked Beans into portions for 1 or 2 and allow to cool and then seal and freeze. To reheat, thoroughly defrost, then either microwave on full for 1-3 mins until hot (dependent on your microwave) or decant into a saucepan and re-warm on the stove top.

Serves: 4 | Ready In: 7 hrs | Per Serving: 148 Calories

BREAKFAST BAKED APPLES V

Ingredients with cals per serving

- 2 (115g/4 oz each once cored) medium red apples, cored – 61 cals
- 2 tsp (6g) raisins – 9 cals
- 2 tsp maple syrup – 13 cals
- 2 tsp (5g) chopped walnuts – 17 cals
- ½ tsp ground cinnamon – 2 cals
- 2 tbsp fat-free, natural fromage frais – 7 cals

Directions

In a bowl, mix together the raisins, walnuts, maple syrup and cinnamon. Core the apples and peel the top third of each apple. Place the apples in the slow cooker and spoon the filling into the cavity of the apples. Carefully pour ½ cup/240ml water around the apples. Set up the slow cooker timer to come onto low 3 ½ hrs before you want to serve the apples (if your slow cooker doesn't have a delayed start function, simply use a plug-in timer attachment to turn on the cooker at the appropriate time).

Serve a hot baked apple with 1 tbsp of 0% fat-free, natural fromage frais per person.

Serves: 2	Ready In: 3-4 hrs	Per Serving: 108 Calories

CODDLED EGGS WITH SOLDIERS V

Ingredients with cals per serving

- 1 slice wholewheat sandwich thin – 50 cals
- 2 UK medium (US large) free range egg – 88 cals
- 2 tsp half fat sour cream – 6 cals
- 2 sprays Frylight olive oil spray – 1 cal
- 2 sage leaves
- pinch kosher/sea salt and freshly grated nutmeg

Directions

Spritz two heat-proof ramekins each with 1 spray of Frylight spray. Spoon 1 tsp of half fat sour cream into the bottom of each ramekin, then crack in a fresh egg. Season with a pinch of Kosher/Sea Salt, a light grating of nutmeg and a sage leaf. Wrap the ramekins with a double layer of kitchen film.

Pour enough boiling water into the slow cooker to reach a depth of 1"/2.5cm. Place the ramekins into the slow cooker. Pop on the lid and cook on high for 1 hour.

When ready to serve, toast the sandwich thin halves, and cut each half into 4 strips (soldiers). Protecting your hands, carefully remove the ramekins from the slow cooker, remove kitchen film, and serve immediately with the "soldiers" on the side.

Serves: 2	Ready In: 1 hr 5	Per Serving: 148 Calories

Soups 100 Calories & Under

Cooking for 1 or 2? Prepare & Store or Freeze Soup Tip: You can store cooled portions of soups from this chapter in the fridge for up to 3 days. Alternatively to keep for longer, freeze individual portions . To serve, defrost then either decant into a saucepan and reheat on the stove top, or microwave on high for 3½ minutes.

Trio of Green Beans and Chicken Soup

Ingredients with cals per serving

- 115g (¾ cup) fresh or frozen baby broad beans – 14 cals
- 115g (¾ cup) frozen edamame soya beans – 21 cals
- 20 fine green beans (120g/4 oz), trimmed – 4 cals
- 2 shallots (100g/½ cup), diced – 3 cals
- 3 garlic cloves, finely chopped – 3 cals
- 2 leeks (white part, 350g/4 cups), sliced – 10 cals
- 150g (1½ cups) fennel – 4 cals
- 3 reduced salt vegetable stock cubes – 11 cals
- 170g (6oz) skinless, cooked chicken breast – 24 cals
- 2 sprays Frylight olive oil spray
- ½ tsp dried thyme

Directions

Remove the frozen beans from the freezer and set aside to slowly defrost whilst the soup is cooking. Dice the shallots and fennel, slice the leeks. If your slow cooker has a sauté function, turn it to that setting otherwise heat a sauté pan over a medium heat. Spritz twice with Frylight spray. Add the shallots, fennel and leeks to the pan and sauté until softened and golden. Finely chop the garlic. Add to the pan and sauté for a further minute. If using a sauté pan, transfer the softened vegetables to slow cooker.

Dissolve the stock cubes in 1.3l /5½ cups of boiling water and add this to the pot along with the dried thyme. Cover with the lid and cook on high for 1 hour. Add the defrosted edamame and broad beans, then allow the stock pot to come back up to a gentle simmer (about 10-15 mins). Taking care with hot liquids, put 2 large ladlefuls of the mixture into a food processor or blender and purée. Return this to the pot and stir. Trim the green beans and cut into 1"/2.5cm pieces. Shred the cooked chicken breast meat. Add the green beans and chicken meat to the stock pot and cook for a further 10-15 mins until the green beans are tender. Season to taste and serve.

A serving is 300g/1¼ cups.

Serves: 8	Ready In: 1½ hrs	Per Serving: 93 Calories

Watercress & Broccoli Soup V

Ingredients with cals per serving

- 150g (5 cups) fresh watercress – 11 cals
- 150g (1 2/3 cups) broccoli stalk – 14 cals
- 1 medium potato, diced (120g/1½ cups) – 25 cals
- 3 tsp vegetable bouillon powder – 10 cals
- ¼ tsp freshly ground black pepper

To serve:

- 60ml (4 tbsp) fat-free, natural fromage frais – 7 cals

Note: This is a great recipe to produce a very low calorie but filling soup and to make sure that the stalk from a head of broccoli doesn't go to waste!

Directions

Trim and discard any really woody pieces from the broccoli stalk, then chop this into small dice. Wash the potato and dice it too (no need to peel). Set aside 4 small sprigs of watercress, then put the diced vegetables and remaining watercress into the slow cooker and season with black pepper. Dissolve the vegetable bouillon powder in 800ml (3¹/₃ cups) of boiling water and pour this over the vegetables. Cover with the slow cooker lid and cook on high for 1½ hrs or on low for 3-4 hrs.

Once cooked, allow the soup to cool slightly, and then liquidise it in batches in a food processor or blender (taking care with liquidising hot liquids). Return the soup to the slow cooker pan and warm through. Season to taste, ladle into soup bowls, swirl in 1 tbsp of fat-free, natural fromage frais into each bowl and garnish with a sprig of watercress.

A serving is 1¼ Cup/300g.

Vegetarian Option: Substitute the Chicken with Quorn Chicken instead.

Serves: 4 Ready In: 1½ - 6 hrs Per Serving: 66 Calories

Ribollita

Ingredients with cals per serving

- 50g (¼ cup) dried cannellini or great northern beans – 28 cals
- 2 Weight Watchers extra trimmed bacon rashers – 18 cals
- ½ medium red onion (40g), diced – 4 cals
- 1 medium carrots (60g), diced – 6 cals
- 70g (2/3 cup) fennel, chopped – 3 cals
- 1 garlic clove – 1 cal
- 200g (7 oz) chopped tinned tomatoes – 13 cals
- 85g (1¼ cups) savoy cabbage, roughly sliced - 7 cals
- 85g (1¼ cups) kale, coarsely chopped – 9 cals
- 1 tsp Herbs de Provence – 1 cals
- 1 reduced salt vegetable stock cube – 8 cals
- ¼ tsp red chilli flakes
- 1 tsp tomato purée – 1 cal
- ½ tsp freshly ground black pepper
- 2 sprays Frylight olive oil spray

Directions

The night before making this soup, rinse the beans and then soak them in 500ml/2 Cups of cold water. Drain and rinse the beans and put them in a large saucepan with a fresh 500ml/2 Cups of water, and bring to a boil and cook uncovered for 10 mins. Set aside.

Dice the onion, carrots and fennel. If your slow cooker has a sauté function, turn it to that setting otherwise heat a sauté pan over a medium heat. Spritz twice with Frylight spray. Sauté the diced vegetables until softened. Slice the bacon into strips. Finely mince the garlic clove and add this along with the bacon to the pan and sauté for a further 2-3 mins. If using the sauté pan, now transfer the softened vegetables to the stock pot. Add the tomatoes, tomato puree, cabbage, kale and herbs to the vegetables in the stock pot and cook on low.

Meanwhile, drain the beans, reserving their cooking liquid. Put half the cooked beans and 60ml/1/4 cup (60ml) cooking liquid into a blender or food processor and liquidise. Add to the slow cooker, along with the remaining whole beans. Dissolve the stock cube in 120ml/ ½ cup of boiling water, then top it up with 240ml/1 cup of the remaining bean cooking liquid. Add to the soup and cook on high (4 hrs) or on low (6 hrs).

A serving is 300g/1¼ cups of soup.

Vegetarian Option: Omit the Bacon.

Serves: 4 Ready In: 4½ - 6½ hrs Per Serving: 97 Calories

Butter Bean & Spiced Pumpkin Soup V

Ingredients with cals per serving

- 600g (5 cups) peeled and deseeded pumpkin (or any other seasonal squash) – 26 cals
- 2 shallots (80g/ ½ cup), diced – 3 cals
- 2 sticks of celery heart (50g/ ½ cup), diced – 1 cal
- 1 red bell pepper (c 150g) – 8 cals
- 1 red chilli, deseeded and minced (c 10g) – 1 cal
- 2 garlic cloves – 1 cal
- 3 reduced salt vegetable stock cubes – 15 cals
- 236g (8 oz) tinned butter beans in water (400g/14oz tin), drained and rinsed – 31 cals
- 15g (1 tbsp) fresh coriander (cilantro), chopped – 1 cal
- ½ tsp sweet smoked paprika – 1 cal
- ½ tsp freshly ground black pepper

Directions

Very carefully, cut the pumpkin into quarters, scoop out and discard the seeds and fibrous centre. Also de-seed the bell pepper and red chilli.

Peel the pumpkin quarters and chop the flesh into 2.5cm/1" chunks. Dice the shallot, celery and red bell pepper. If your slow cooker has a sauté function, turn it to that setting otherwise heat a sauté pan over a medium heat. Spritz twice with Frylight spray and sauté the shallot, celery and red bell pepper for 5 mins. Add the pumpkin and sauté for 2-3 mins. Finely chop the chilli and garlic, add this to the pan and cook for a further minute. If using a sauté pan, transfer the softened vegetables to the slow cooker.

Dissolve the stock cubes in 1ltr (4 cups) of boiling water and add to the slow cooker along with the paprika and black pepper. Cover with the lid and cook on high for 3 hrs or on slow for 6 hrs. Taking care with hot liquids, transfer to a liquidiser or food processor in batches and whizz until smooth. Return the soup to the slow cooker. Stir in the coriander (cilantro) and the drained, rinsed butter beans, cook for a further 15 minutes until the beans are warmed through. Season to taste and serve. A serving is 300g/1¼ cups.

Serves: 6	Ready In: 3½ hrs	Per Serving: 89 Calories

Autumn Harvest Festival Soup V

Ingredients with cals per serving

- 400g (14 oz) chopped tinned tomatoes – 17 cals
- 1 medium red onion (80g/ ½ cup), diced – 5 cals
- 2 sticks of celery heart (50g/ ½ cup), diced – 1 cal
- 2 medium carrots (120g/1 cup), diced – 7 cals
- 1 medium parsnip (115g/ ¾ cup), diced – 14 cals
- 1 tsp fresh ginger, peeled and grated – 1 cals
- 115g (¾ cup) sweet potato, peeled and chopped weight – 19 cals
- 145g (1¼ cups) butternut squash, peeled and chopped weight – 10 cals
- 130g (1 cup) celeriac/jicama, peeled and chopped weight – 5 cals
- 1 garlic clove, minced – 1 cals
- 1 tbsp honey – 8 cals
- ½ tsp paprika
- 2 reduced salt vegetable stock cubes – 10 cals
- 2 sprays Frylight olive oil spray
- ½ tsp freshly ground black pepper
- 6 tsp fat-free, natural fromage frais – 2 cals

Directions

Dice the onion, carrots and celery. If your slow cooker has a sauté function, turn it to that setting otherwise heat a sauté pan over a medium heat. Spritz twice with Frylight spray and sauté the onions, celery and carrots for 5 mins. Finely mince the garlic and grate the ginger root and add to the pan along with the paprika and black pepper, cook for a further 1 minute. If using a sauté pan, transfer the softened vegetables to the slow cooker. Peel and chop the sweet potato, jicama/celeriac, butternut squash and parsnip. Add to the slow cooker along with the chopped tomatoes and give everything a good stir.

Dissolve the stock cubes in 0.75ltr (3¼ cups) of boiling water and add to the slow cooker, along with the honey. Cover with the lid and cook on high for 3 hrs or on slow for 6 hrs.

Once cooked, allow the soup to cool slightly, and then liquidise it in batches in a food processor or blender (taking care with liquidising hot liquids). Return the soup to the slow cooker pan and warm through. Season to taste, ladle into soup bowls, garnishing each bowl with 1 tsp of fat-free, natural fromage frais. A serving is 300g/1¼ cups.

Serves: 6	Ready In: 3½ hrs	Per Serving: 100 Calories

Creamy Mushroom & Garlic Soup V

Ingredients with cals per serving

- 480g (4 cups) baby chestnut (portabella) mushrooms – 19 cals
- 25g (1 oz) dried wild mushrooms – 12 cals
- 2 leeks (white part, 350g/ 4 cups), sliced – 20 cals
- 1 small garlic bulb – 10 cals
- ¾ cup (180ml) semi-skimmed (reduced fat) milk – 23 cals
- 1 reduced salt vegetable stock cube – 8 cals
- 3 sprigs fresh thyme
- 2 sprays Frylight olive oil spray – 1 cal
- 2 tbsp (30ml) fat-free, natural fromage frais – 3 cals
- ½ tsp freshly ground black pepper

Directions

In a heatproof bowl or jug, cover the dried mushrooms with 400ml (1 2/3 cups) of boiling water. Give them a stir and set aside to soak for 15 mins. Meanwhile, peel the cloves from the garlic bulb but just leave them whole. Don't be alarmed at the amount of garlic, slow cooking whole cloves of garlic gives a lovely mellow flavour.

Clean then slice the chestnut (baby portabella) mushrooms. Cut the leeks in half lengthwise and rinse to remove any residual grit. Thinly slice. If your slow cooker has a sauté function, turn it to that setting otherwise heat a sauté pan over a medium heat. Spritz twice with Frylight spray and sauté the sliced leeks for 5 mins. Add the fresh mushrooms and continue to cook for a further 5 mins, turning occasionally. Finally, add the whole garlic cloves and sauté for 2 mins. If using a sauté pan, transfer the softened vegetables to the slow cooker.

Line a sieve with kitchen towel and use this to drain the liquid from the soaking mushrooms into slow cooker, pressing the wild mushrooms to extract as much of their liquor as possible. Remove the wild mushrooms from the sieve (discarding the kitchen towel and any grit that came from the wild mushrooms). Finely chop the soaked wild mushrooms and add to the slow cooker, along with the black pepper, sprigs of thyme and stock cube.

Cover with the lid and cook on slow for 6 hrs. Allow to cool slightly and remove the thyme stalks. Then taking care with hot liquids, transfer to a liquidiser or food processor in batches and whizz in until smooth. It will be a thick puree at this point. Return the puree to slow cooker. Stir in enough of the milk to slacken the soup to your preferred thickness. Reheat until warmed through completely and check the seasoning. Serve in warmed bowls, topped with ½ tbsp of fat-free, natural fromage frais per serving. A serving is 300g/1¼ cups.

Serves: 4	Ready In: 7 hrs	Per Serving: 95 Calories

Minted Pea & Leek Soup V

Ingredients with cals per serving

- 15oz (425g) frozen petits pois – 65 cals
- 1 leek (175g/2 cups) – 12 cals
- 2 sticks of celery (50g/½ cup) – 1 cal
- 2 garlic cloves, minced – 2 cals
- 2 reduced salt vegetable stock cubes – 15 cals
- 2 sprays Frylight olive oil spray
- 2 tbsp fresh mint, chopped – 2 cals
- 4 tsp 0% fat plain fromage frais– 2 cals

Directions

Split the leek in half lengthwise and rinse thoroughly to remove any grit. De-thread the celery stalks by running a vegetable peeler over the ribbed side. Dice the leek and celery. If your slow cooker has a sauté function, turn it to that setting otherwise heat a sauté pan over a medium heat.

Spritz twice with Frylight spray and sauté the celery and leek. Sauté for 7 mins until softened. Finely mince the garlic cloves and add these to the pan and cook for a further minute. If using the sauté pan, transfer the softened veg to the slow cooker.

Meanwhile, dissolve the stock cubes in 2½ Cups (0.6ltr) of boiling water. Add the stock to the slow cooker, along with the frozen peas. Cover with the lid and cook for 1½ hrs (high) or 3½ hrs (slow).

Remove the slow cooker insert from the heat, add the chopped mint and allow the soup to cool slightly. Then liquidise it in batches in a food processor or blender (taking care with liquidising hot liquids). Return the soup to a slow cooker and warm through. Season to taste, ladle into soup bowls, garnishing each bowl with 1 tsp fat-free, natural fromage frais. A serving is 1¼ cup/300g.

Serves: 4 | Ready In: 2-4 hrs | Per Serving: 85 Calories

5:2 Salt & Cracked Black Pepper Croutons V

Ingredients with cals per serving

- 2 slices calorie controlled whole-wheat bread eg Weight Watchers – 18 cals
- 4 sprays Frylight olive oil spray
- ½ tsp sea salt
- ½ tsp coarsely ground black pepper

Directions

Preheat the oven to 180C fan, 400F, Gas Mark 6. Line a baking sheet with baking parchment.

Meanwhile, cut each bread slice into 4 strips and then cut each strip into 4 cubes. Spread over the baking sheet, spritz with 2 sprays of Frylight spray and season with coarsely ground black pepper and sea salt. Give them a good toss, spritz with 2 further sprays of Frylight spray and put in the oven. After 5 mins, toss again and return to the oven for a further 5-10 mins until golden and crispy. When cooked, carefully remove the croutons on the parchment from the baking sheet to prevent the croutons cooking any further and allow to cool. A serving is 4 croutons.

Serves: 8	Ready In: 20 mins	Per Serving: 18 Calories

5:2 Baked Garlic & Rosemary Croutons V

Ingredients with cals per serving

- 2 slices calorie controlled whole-wheat bread eg Weight Watchers – 18 cals
- 4 sprays Frylight olive oil spray – 1 cal
- 2 garlic cloves
- 1 tsp dried rosemary

Directions

Preheat the oven to 180C fan, 400F, Gas Mark 6. Line a baking sheet with baking parchment.

Meanwhile, cut each bread slice into 4 strips and then cut each strip into 4 cubes. Spread over the baking sheet, spritz with 2 sprays of Frylight spray then grate over the garlic cubes and sprinkle with the dried rosemary. Give them a good toss, spritz with 2 further sprays of Frylight spray and put in the oven. After 5 mins, toss again and return to the oven for a further 5-10 mins until golden and crispy. When cooked, carefully remove the croutons on the parchment from the baking sheet to prevent the croutons cooking any further and allow to cool. A serving is 4 croutons.

Serves: 8	Ready In: 20 mins	Per Serving: 20 Calories

5:2 Oven-Baked Tomato & Basil Croutons V

Ingredients with cals per serving

- 2 slices calorie controlled whole-wheat bread eg Weight Watchers – 18 cals
- 4 sprays Frylight olive oil spray – 1 cal
- 2 tsp tomato purée – 1 cal
- 1 tsp dried basil

Directions

Preheat the oven to 180C fan, 400F, Gas Mark 6. Line a baking sheet with baking parchment.

Meanwhile, spread each bread slice with ½ tsp of tomato purée, then turn over and spread over another ½ tsp of tomato purée. Cut each bread slice into 4 strips and then cut each strip into 4 cubes. Spread over the baking sheet, spritz with 2 sprays of Frylight spray then sprinkle with the dried basil. Give them a good toss, spritz with 2 further sprays of Frylight spray and put in the oven. After 5 mins, toss again and return to the oven for a further 5-10 mins until golden and crispy. When cooked, carefully remove the croutons on the parchment from the baking sheet to prevent the croutons cooking any further and allow to cool. A serving is 4 croutons.

Serves: 8	Ready In: 20 mins	Per Serving: 20 Calories

Cooking for 1 or 2? Prepare & Store or Freeze Tip: You can store cooled croutons in a sealable airtight container and store in the fridge for up to 3 days. Alternatively, freeze, then defrost before use.

Soups 150 Calories & Under

Cooking for 1 or 2? Prepare & Store or Freeze Soup Tip: You can store cooled portions of soups from this chapter in te fridge for up to 3 days. Alternatively to keep for longer, freeze individual portions . To serve, defrost then either decant into a saucepan and reheat on the stove top, or microwave on high for 3½ minutes.

Mexican Chicken Soup

Ingredients with cals per serving

- 125g (4½ oz) boneless, skinless chicken breast – 35 cals
- 100g (½ cup) dried pinto beans – 30 cals
- 1 white onion (80g/½ cup), diced – 8 cals
- 1½ medium celery stalk (60g/4 tbsp), diced – 2 cals
- 1½ medium carrots (90g/¾ cup), diced – 8 cals
- 2 garlic cloves – 2 cals
- 2 reduced salt chicken stock cubes – 15 cals
- 200g (7 oz) tin chopped tomatoes – 13 cals
- 1 green chilli (10g) – 2 cals
- ½ tsp ground cumin – 1 cal
- ½ tsp ground coriander – 1 cal
- 1 tbsp fresh cilantro/coriander – 1 cal
- 1 dash Tabasco sauce
- ½ tsp freshly ground black pepper
- 1 whole-wheat mini tortilla wrap – 24 cals
- 1 lime – 5 cals
- 2 sprays Frylight olive oil spray

Directions

The night before making this soup, rinse the beans and then soak them in 2 cups (500ml) of cold water. Drain and rinse, then put the rinsed beans in a saucepan with 2 cups (500ml) of fresh cold water, bring to a rapid boil and cook for 10 minutes. Then drain and rinse again.

Meanwhile, dice the onion, carrots and celery. If your slow cooker has a sauté function, turn it to that setting otherwise heat a sauté pan over a medium heat. Spritz twice with Frylight spray and sauté the onion, carrots and celery for 7 mins until softened. Remove the leaves from the fresh cilantro/coriander and store in a sealed container in the fridge. Deseed the green chillies and finely mince along with the garlic cloves and the fresh cilantro/coriander stalks. Add these to the pan and cook for a further minute.

Finally, add the ground coriander, cumin and black pepper and cook for 1 minute to release the fragrance from the spices. If using the sauté pan, transfer the softened vegetables to the slow cooker. Tuck the chicken breast in amongst the vegetables. Dissolve the stock cubes in 840ml/3½ cups of boiling water and add to the pan along with the chopped tomatoes and drained pinto beans and a dash or two of Tabasco Sauce. Cover with the lid and cook on low for 8 hrs.

Meanwhile, preheat the oven to 160C fan, 350F, Gas Mark 4. Line a baking sheet with parchment. Cut the tortilla in ½, then cut it crosswise into 1cm strips. Spread the strips over the baking sheet and pop into the oven. Bake until toasted (watch very carefully) about 5 mins. When the soup is cooked, use a slotted spoon to carefully remove the chicken to a plate and shred the meat. Return to the soup and squeeze in the juice from the lime. Give everything a good stir. Roughly chop the reserved coriander/cilantro leaves. To serve, ladle into a bowl and sprinkle over the chopped herbs and baked tortilla strips. A serving is 300g/1¼ cups.

Cooking for 1 or 2? Prepare & Store or Freeze Soup Tip:

Freeze the baked tortilla strips separately in a freezer bag. Defrost before sprinkling on top of the hot soup.

Serves: 4	Ready In: 8 hrs	Per Serving: 145 Calories

London Particular Soup V

Ingredients with cals per serving

- 175g (¾ cup + 2 tbsp) dried yellow split peas, rinsed – 88 cals
- ½ medium onion (40g/¼ cup), diced – 4 cals
- 1 medium leek (175g/2 cups), trimmed – 12 cals
- 1 medium celery stalk (40g/3 tbsp), diced – 1 cal
- 1 large carrot (60g/½ cup), diced – 6 cals
- 1 bay leaves
- 2 sprigs thyme
- ¼ tsp freshly ground black pepper
- 2 vegetable stock cubes – 15 cals

Directions

Dice the onion, leek, celery and carrot. Rinse the split peas and add to the slow cooker along with the diced vegetables. Dissolve the stock cubes in 840ml/3½ cups of boiling water. Add to the pot along with the herbs and freshly ground black pepper. Cover with the lid and cook on a low heat for 3½ -4 hrs.

When the split peas are cooked and very tender, remove the bay leaves and thyme stalks. Allow the soup to cool slightly, then liquidise in batches in a food processor or liquidiser (taking great care with hot liquids) and process until the soup is smooth. Add some boiling water if the soup is too thick. Check the seasoning, and then serve in hot bowls. A serving is 300g/1¼ cups.

Serves: 4 | Ready In: 4 hrs | Per Serving: 125 Calories

Lentil & Sweet Potato Soup (V)

Ingredients with cals per serving

- 250g (1¾ cups) sweet potato, peeled and diced – 61 cals
- 75g (6 tbsp) dried red or yellow lentils, rinsed and drained – 38 cals
- 2 medium carrots (120g/1 cup) – 11 cals
- 1 medium leek (175g/2 cups), sliced – 12 cals
- 2 medium sticks of celery heart (80g/ ¾ cup), diced – 2 cals
- 2 garlic cloves – 2 cals
- 2 tbsp fresh ginger, peeled and grated – 1 cal
- 1 tsp ground coriander
- 1 tsp ground cumin
- ½ tsp ground turmeric
- ½ tsp red chilli flakes
- 2 reduced salt vegetable stock cubes – 15 cals
- 2 sprays Frylight olive oil spray
- ½ tsp freshly ground black pepper
- 10g (½ cup) fresh coriander/ cilantro – 1 cal

Directions

Split the leek in half lengthwise and rinse to remove any grit, then pat dry and slice. Dice the sweet potato (no need to peel, just scrub clean), carrots and celery. If your stockpot has a sauté function, spritz with 2 sprays of Frylight olive oil spray and sauté the prepared vegetables until softened. Otherwise, spritz a sauté pan with the olive oil spray, then sauté the vegetables.

Separate the leaves from the stalks of the cilantro/coriander. Pop the leaves into a sealable container and put into the fridge for later. Finely chop the stalks along with the garlic, then grate the fresh ginger. Add all these to the pan and cook for a further minute, then add the spices, stir and cook for another minute to release the spicy fragrance, stirring to prevent the mixture from sticking. If using a sauté pan, now transfer everything to the slow cooker.

Dissolve the stock cubes in 750ml/3 Cups of boiling water and add to the slow cooker along with the rinsed and drained red lentils. Give everything a good stir then cover and cook on low for 7 ½ hrs.

Before serving, whisk the cooked soup and thin with boiling water if too thick for your liking and season to taste. Roughly chop the reserved coriander/cilantro leaves. Serve in warm bowls with the chopped herbs sprinkled over the top. A serving is 350g/1½ Cups.

Serves: 4	Ready In: 8 hrs	Per Serving: 148 Calories

Creamy Fish Chowder

Ingredients with cals per serving

- 115g (4oz) cooked shrimp/prawns – 24 cals
- 115g (4oz) fillet smoked haddock or other smoked white fish – 23 cals
- 80g (½ cup) frozen sweetcorn – 23 cals
- 1 Weight Watchers extra trimmed bacon rasher – 9 cals
- 100g (1⅓ cups) waxy potatoes such as Charlotte or Yukon gold, cubed – 19 cals
- ¾ medium leek (90g/1½ cups), sliced – 9 cals
- 75g (¾ cup) fennel, chopped – 3 cals
- 300ml (1 ¼ cup) fresh skimmed (fat free) milk – 26 cals
- 1 reduced salt vegetable stock cube – 8 cals
- 2 tsp corn starch (cornflour) – 4 cals
- 1 bay leaf
- 2 sprigs fresh thyme or lemon thyme
- pinch sea (kosher) salt
- ½ tsp freshly ground black pepper
- 3 sprays Frylight olive oil spray

Directions

Cut the leek in half lengthwise and rinse well to remove any grit. Pat dry and thickly slice. Dice the fennel. Cut the bacon rasher into strips. If your slow cooker has a sauté function, turn it to that setting otherwise heat a sauté pan over a medium heat. Spritz with 1 spray of Frylight spray and add the bacon strips and sauté until crisp. Remove with a slotted spoon and reserve. Spritz the pan with two further sprays of Frylight olive oil spray and add the leek and fennel to the pan. Turn the heat to low and sauté for about 7 mins until softened.

If using the sauté pan, transfer the softened vegetables to the slow cooker. Dice the potatoes into cubes and add these to the slow cooker along with the freshly ground black pepper. Dissolve the vegetable stock cube into 300ml/1 ¼ cup of boiling water and add to the crockpot along with the sweetcorn kernels, bay leaf and thyme sprigs. Cover with the lid and cook on low for 3 hrs.

After 3 hrs, dissolve the cornstarch/cornflour in the milk and add this to the slow cooker, give everything a good stir and then place the haddock fillet on top of the vegetables and poach for 30 mins. Using a slotted spoon, remove from the haddock from slow cooker. Carefully, remove any skin and bones from the haddock fillet, then flake into bite size pieces and return to the pan along with the cooked prawns/shrimp and bacon strips. Cook for a further 10-15 mins until heated through. Remove the thyme stalks and serve the chowder in warmed bowls. A serving is 300g/1¼ cups.

Serves: 4	Ready In: 4 hrs	Per Serving: 149 Calories

Tuscan Bean & Rosemary Soup (V)

Ingredients with cals per serving

- 1 cup (200g) dried white cannellini beans – 113 cals
- 1 white onion – 8 cals
- ¾ cup (75g) fennel, diced – 3 cals
- 2 sprays Frylight olive oil spray – 1 cal
- 2 garlic cloves – 2 cals
- 2 reduced salt vegetable stock cubes – 15 cals
- 1 bay leaves
- 2 sprigs fresh rosemary – 1 cal
- 2 sprigs of fresh thyme 1 cal
- pinch freshly ground black pepper

Directions

The night before making this soup, rinse the beans and then soak them in 2 cups (500ml) of cold water. Drain and rinse, then put the rinsed beans in a saucepan with 2 cups (500ml) of fresh cold water, bring to a rapid boil and cook for 10 minutes. Then drain and rinse again.

Meanwhile, set aside 1 sprig of Rosemary and then tie the remainder of the herbs together with a piece of kitchen string to create a bouquet garni. Dissolve the stock cubes in 3 ¾ Cups (900ml) of boiling water. Dice the onion and fennel bulb. If your stockpot has a sauté function, spritz with 2 sprays of Frylight olive oil spray and sauté the onion and fennel until softened. Otherwise, spritz a sauté pan with the olive oil spray, then sauté the vegetables.

Finely mince the garlic and add to the onion/fennel and cook for a further 1 minute. If using a sauté pan, transfer the sautéed vegetables to the slow cooker. Then add the drained, rinsed beans, bouquet garni, black pepper and stock. Give everything a good stir. Cover with a lid on and cook on low for 8 hrs.

When the beans are ready, remove the bouquet garni, allow the soup to cool slightly, and then liquidise it in batches in a food processor or blender (taking care with liquidising hot liquids). Check the seasoning and re-warm. Remove the leaves from the reserved sprig of rosemary and finely mince. Ladle the soup into warm bowls and sprinkle over the rosemary. A serving is 240g/1 cup.

Serves: 6	Ready In: 8 hrs	Per Serving: 130 Calories

Cauliflower & Stilton Soup V

Ingredients with cals per serving

- 600g (5 ½ cups) cauliflower (c. 1 medium cauliflower) – 38 cals
- 57g (2 oz) stilton cheese – 39 cals
- 300ml (1¼ cup) skimmed (low fat) milk – 18 cals
- 2 bay leaves
- 3 medium stalks of celery heart (120g/1¼ cup), diced – 2 cals
- 2 medium leeks, trimmed (350g/4 cups), sliced – 16 cals
- 1 medium white potato (110g/4oz), diced – 15 cals
- 30ml (2 tbsp) fat-free, natural fromage frais – 2 cals
- 2 sprays Frylight olive oil spray
- 2 reduced salt vegetable stock cubes – 10 cals
- ½ tsp freshly ground black pepper

Directions

Split the leeks in half lengthwise and rinse thoroughly to remove any grit. De-thread the celery stalks by running a vegetable peeler over the ribbed side. Dice the leek and celery. If your stockpot has a sauté function, spritz with 2 sprays of Frylight olive oil spray and sauté the prepared vegetables until softened. Otherwise, spritz a sauté pan with the olive oil spray, then sauté the vegetables.

Don't peel the potato, just dice it. Break off the cauliflower florets, and chop into even sized pieces. Finely dice the cauliflower stalk and any small, crisp inner leaves. Add to the pan and sauté for 2-3 mins. If using a sauté pan, now transfer everything back to the slow cooker.

Dissolve the stock cubes in 2 cups (450mls) of boiling water and add to the slow cooker along with the milk, bay leaves and freshly ground black pepper. Cover with the lid and cook on low for 4-6 hrs.

Remove the bay leaves from the slow cooker and discard. Allow the soup to cool slightly, then liquidise in batches in a food processor or liquidiser (taking great care with hot liquids) and process until the soup is smooth and creamy. Return to the slow cooker for 10-15 mins to thorough re-warm through. Stir in the fromage frais and stilton cheese and keep stirring until the cheese has melted and the soup is hot. Check the seasoning, and then serve in hot bowls.

A serving is 1¼ cup/300g.

Serves: 6	Ready In: 4½ - 6½ hrs	Per Serving: 140 Calories

Meals 200 Calories & Under

Coconut Prawn & Spinach Dahl

Ingredients with cals per serving

- 100g (3½ oz) raw shrimp/king prawns – 33 cals
- 30g (2 tbsp + 1 tsp) red lentils, dry weight, rinsed – 30 cals
- 9 cherry tomatoes (100g) - 10 cals
- 90g (3 cups) baby spinach – 14 cals
- 1 red onion (80g), diced – 16 cals
- ½ red bell pepper – 13 cals
- 150ml (½ cup + 2 tbsp) reduced fat coconut milk – 55 cals
- 2 tsp medium strength curry powder – 6 cals
- ½ tbsp freshly grated ginger – 2 cals
- 1 garlic clove – 2 cals
- 1 red chilli (10g) – 3 cals
- 2 tbsp chopped fresh coriander – 2 cals
- ½ lime – 5 cals
- pinch sea (kosher) salt
- pinch ground black pepper
- 2 sprays Frylight olive oil spray – 1 cal
- 2 tbsp (30ml) 0% Greek yogurt – 9 cal

Directions

Cut the red onion in half and finely slice. Remove the seeds and pith from the red pepper and red chilli. Cut the pepper into thick slices. Finely mince the red chilli with the garlic clove. If your stockpot has a sauté function, spritz with 2 sprays of Frylight spray. Otherwise, heat a non-stick sauté pan over a medium heat and spritz with the olive oil spray. Add the onion and red pepper slices and cook for 5 mins until softened and golden. Meanwhile, remove the skins from the tomatoes by placing them in a heat proof bowl and covering with boiling water for 1 min. Carefully remove from the water with a slotted spoon, and when cool enough to handle, slip off the skins and discard.

Returning your attention to the pan, add the minced garlic and chilli and the grated ginger and cook for a further minute. Then add the curry powder and stir around the pan to release the fragrance of the spices. If using a sauté pan, now transfer everything to the slow cooker. Add the coconut milk, rinsed red lentils and tomatoes, give everything a good stir, then cover and cook on low for 4 hrs. After 4 hrs, stir the spinach and prawns into the curry and cook for a further 10 mins until the prawns are pink and cooked through and the spinach has wilted. Ladle into warm bowls, sprinkle with freshly chopped coriander, add a tbsp of 0% Fat Greek yogurt and squeeze over the juice of a ¼ lime.

Cooking for 1? Prepare & Store or Freeze Meal Tip: You can store cooled portions of dahl, before adding the spinach and prawns, in a sealed container in the fridge for up to 3 days. Alternatively, freeze individual portions, again before adding the spinach and prawns, then defrost before use. Either decant into a saucepan and reheat on the stove top, or microwave on high for 3½ minutes to serve. Once the dahl is reheated, stir in the spinach and prawns and reheat to wilt the spinach and cook the prawns.

Serves: 2	Ready In: 4½ hrs	Per Serving: 191 Calories

MEATBALLS

Ingredients with cals per serving

- 170g (6oz) ground, minced turkey breast – 43 cals
- 115g (4oz) ground, minced extra lean beef – 32 cals
- 2 tbsp (12.5g) finely grated fresh parmesan – 12 cals
- 165g (1⅓ cup) chestnut (portabella) mushrooms – 6 cals
- ½ tbsp mixed dried herbs – 1 cal
- 2 garlic cloves, divided – 2 cals
- 1 tsp red chilli flakes, divided – 2 cals
- ½ small slice calorie-controlled brown bread – 9 cals
- 1 tbsp semi-skimmed (reduced fat) milk – 2 cals
- 1 carrot (60g), grated – 6 cals
- 2 shallots, divided – 5 cals
- 1 celery stalk (40g), divided – 1 cal
- 1 egg white – 4 cals
- 6 sprays Frylight olive oil spray – 2 cals
- 400g (14 oz) tinned chopped tomatoes – 25 cals
- 2 tbsp chopped fresh basil – 1 cal
- 1 small cauliflower (520g) – 49 cal or 6 oz (180g) wholewheat spaghetti – 140 cal
- ¼ tsp freshly ground black pepper
- ⅛ tsp sea (kosher) salt

Directions

In a mini-food processor, process the bread into crumbs and place in a small bowl. Add 1 tbsp milk, stir to coat all the crumbs with milk then set aside to soak. Very finely mince ½ of one of the shallots, 1/3 of the celery stalk plus the stalks from the mushrooms. Heat a non-stick sauté pan over a medium heat and spritz twice with Frylight. Add the minced shallot, celery and mushrooms to the pan and sauté for 5 minutes until softened, stirring occasionally. Grate the carrot and add this to the pan, cook for a further 2 mins. Finely mince 1 garlic clove and add to the vegetables and cook for 1 min. Empty into a large bowl and allow to cool. Wipe out the sauté pan. Cut the remaining shallots in halves lengthwise, then finely slice along with the remaining celery stalk. Slice the mushroom caps. Re-heat the sauté pan over a medium heat and spritz with a further 2 sprays of Frylight spray. Add the sliced shallots and celery and sauté for 5 minutes until softened, stirring occasionally. Add the sliced mushrooms and continue to sauté until slightly golden. Finely mince the remaining garlic clove and add this to the sauté pan, cook for a further minute. Empty into the slow cooker and add the chopped tomatoes, along with ½ tsp of red chilli flakes, 1 tsp of dried herbs salt and pepper. Stir and put the lid on, cook on high whilst you finish preparing the meatballs. Wipe out the sauté pan again.

In the bowl with the sautéed vegetables, add the 2 meats, ½ tsp each of dried herbs and of chilli flakes, along with the milk-soaked breadcrumbs, grated parmesan and egg white. Mix well to combine (clean hands work best!) Use your hands to create 20 meatballs from the mixture. Re-heat the sauté pan over a medium heat and spritz twice with Frylight. Fry the meatballs in 2 batches, turning until golden and crispy on the outside, and then add to the sauce in the slow cooker. Cover with the lid and turn the cooker to slow. Cook for 6 hrs.

To serve with spaghetti, bring a large saucepan of lightly salted water to the boil and cook the spaghetti according to the packet instructions for al dente. Shred the fresh basil leaves. When the spaghetti is cooked, drain, retaining a couple of tbsp of the cooking liquid. Divide the spaghetti between 4 warm pasta bowls, and spoon over the meatballs. Check the consistency of the remaining sauce and add enough of the reserved pasta cooking liquid to bring the sauce to the consistency you like. Spoon over the tomato and mushroom sauce, scatter over the chopped basil and serve.

To serve with cauliflower 'cous cous', divide the cauliflower into florets and then roughly chop along with the stalk. Transfer to a food processor (don't overfill, divide into 2 or more batches if necessary) and pulse until the consistency of cous cous. Empty out into a bowl and return any larger pieces to the processor to pulse again. Re-heat the sauté pan over a medium heat and spritz twice Frylight, add the cauliflower and season with salt and pepper. Cook for 5 to 8 mins, until the cous cous is tender. Shred the fresh basil leaves. When the cous cous is cooked, divide between 4 warm pasta bowls, and spoon over the meatballs. Check the consistency of the remaining sauce and add enough boiling water to bring the sauce to the thickness you like. Spoon over the sauce, scatter over the chopped basil and serve.

Cooking for 1 or 2? Prepare & Freeze Meal Tip:

Cook all the tomato sauce and meatballs but only enough spaghetti or cous cous for how much you want to eat straight away. Before serving, divide the cooked tomato sauce and meatballs into individual portions into freezer foil trays with lids. Seal with the tray lid and freeze. To reheat, thoroughly defrost, remove tray lid and then bake in a preheated oven (160C fan, 350F, Gas Mark 4) for 20 mins, cooking a fresh portion of spaghetti/cous cous to go with it.

With cauliflower cous cous

Serves: 4	Ready In: 6½ hrs	Per Serving: 200 Calories

With spaghetti

Serves: 4	Ready In: 6½ hrs	Per Serving: 291 Calories

Sun-dried Tomato Humous with Vegetable Crudités (V)

Ingredients with cals per serving

- 30g (1 oz) sun-dried tomatoes (not in oil) – 10 cals
- 80g (1/3 cup + 1 tbsp) dried chickpeas – 71 cals
- 8 garlic cloves – 7 cals
- 18g (2 tbsp) sesame seeds – 28 cals
- 80g (1/3 cup) 0% Greek yogurt – 11 cals
- 1 reduced salt vegetable stock cube – 8 cals
- 1 lemon, squeezed, divided – 5 cals
- ½ tsp ground cumin – 1 cal
- ¼ tsp ground coriander – 1 cal
- 16 baby corn (150g) – 11 cals
- 1 red pepper – 13 cals
- 4 medium carrots (240g) – 22 cals
- ¼ tsp fresh ground black pepper
- 1/8 tsp sea (kosher) salt

Directions

Soak the dried chickpeas overnight in 2 cups of cold water, then drain and rinse.

Heat a non-stick sauté pan over a medium heat and add the sesame seeds. Cook until toasted and lightly golden (about 5 mins but don't leave them unattended as they'll quickly burn). As soon as they are toasted, remove from the pan and allow to cool. Transfer to a mini-food processor and grind for 2-3 mins.

Squeeze in the juice of ½ a lemon (reserve the remaining half for later) and process again for 1-2 mins. You should now have a sesame paste. Scrap this into the slow cooker and add the sun-dried tomatoes, rinsed and drained chickpeas, garlic cloves, cumin and coriander. Dissolve the vegetable stock cube in 240ml (1 cup) boiling water and add to the slow cooker. Cover with the lid and cook on low for 8 hrs.

Drain the cooked chickpeas, but reserve the cooking liquid. Allow to cool, then transfer to a food processor, along with the Greek yogurt, juice from the reserved half lemon, salt and pepper. Process into a rough paste. If the paste is too thick, add a splash or two of the reserved cooking liquid Divide into 4 individual ramekins and chill for 2 hours before serving.

To serve, de-seed the pepper, remove any pith and cut into juicy strips. Cut the carrots into batons. Serve the Humous with the crudités to the side.

Cooking for 1 or 2? Prepare & Store Meal Tip: You can store this humous in a sealable airtight container and store in the fridge for up to 3 days.

Serves: 4 | Ready In: 7½ - 8 hrs | Per Serving: 187 Calories

Chickpea, Spinach & Mushroom Goan Curry

V

Ingredients with cals per serving

- 40g (3 tbsp) dried chickpeas, soaked overnight – 71 cals
- 2 medium tomatoes (160g), roughly chopped – 16 cals
- 1 red onion (80g) – 16 cals
- 200g (2⅓ cups) baby chestnut (baby bella) mushrooms – 16 cals
- 90g (3 cups) baby spinach – 14 cals
- 2 garlic cloves – 4 cals
- 1 red chilli (10g) – 3 cals
- 2 tbsp fresh ginger, finely chopped – 3 cals
- ½ reduced salt vegetable stock cubes – 8 cals
- 120ml (½ cup) light coconut milk – 44 cals
- 2 sprays Frylight olive oil spray – 1 cal
- ½ tsp paprika – 2 cals
- ¼ tsp ground turmeric – 1 cal
- 1 tsp ground coriander – 5 cals
- ½ tsp ground cumin – 2 cals
- ½ tsp cayenne pepper – 2 cals
- pinch freshly ground black pepper, divided
- pinch sea (kosher) salt, divided
- 20g (4 tsp) 0% Greek yogurt – 6 cals

Directions

Soak the dried chickpeas overnight in 2 cups of cold water, then drain and rinse.

Dice the red onion. If your slow cooker has a sauté function, spritz with 2 sprays of Frylight olive oil spray. Otherwise, heat a non-stick sauté pan over a medium heat and spritz with the olive oil spray. Add the onion and sauté for 7 minutes until softened, stirring occasionally. Clean the baby mushrooms and add the pan. Continue to sauté until they turn a light golden colour (about another 7 mins). Deseed the chilli and thinly slice and finely mince the garlic and peeled fresh ginger. Add to the pan and cook for 1 min. Stir in the spices, salt and pepper, stirring until the spices are warmed and their fragrance is released. If using a sauté pan, decant the sautéed vegetables to the slow cooker.

Dissolve the ½ stock cube in ½ cup/120ml of boiling water and add to the sautéed vegetables, along with the drained chickpeas, chopped tomatoes and coconut milk. Cover with the slow cooker lid and cook on low for 7-8 hrs. When ready to serve, stir in the baby spinach until wilted, then serve in warm bowls, topped with 2 tsp of 0% Greek yogurt.

Cooking for 1 or 2? Prepare & Freeze Meal Tip:

Before stirring in the spinach, divide the Curry into individual portions into freezer foil trays with lids. Seal with the tray lid and freeze. To reheat, thoroughly defrost, loosen the tray lid and then bake in a preheated oven (160C fan, 350F, Gas Mark 4) for 20 mins, stir in a fresh portion of spinach to go with it.

Serves: 2 | Ready In: 7½ - 8 hrs | Per Serving: 200 Calories

Stuffed Peppers

Ingredients with cals per serving

- 2 red or yellow peppers – 50 cals
- 25g (2 tbsp) dry brown basmati rice – 44 cals
- 115g (4 oz) minced (ground) turkey breast – 58 cals
- 200g (7oz) chopped tomatoes – 25 cals
- 85g (1 cup) baby chestnut (baby bella) mushrooms – 7 cals
- ½ shallot (40g), finely chopped – 5 cals
- 1 garlic clove – 2 cals
- 1 stick celery heart (20g), finely chopped – 1 cal
- ½ tsp Herb de Provence – 1 cal
- 1 tsp tomato purée – 3 cals
- 2 sprays Frylight olive oil spray – 1 cal
- pinch freshly ground black pepper, divided
- pinch sea (kosher) salt, divided

Directions

Neatly cut the tops off the peppers and set aside (you are going to use them as lids to your stuffed peppers). Carefully remove and discard the seeds and ribs from inside the peppers. Check that they can stand upright, if necessary, trim a little off the base to make them stable. Finely dice the shallot and celery. If your stockpot has a sauté function, spritz with 2 sprays of Frylight olive oil spray. Otherwise, heat a non-stick sauté pan over a medium heat and spritz with the olive oil spray. Add the shallot and celery and sauté for 7 minutes until softened, stirring occasionally. Clean the baby mushrooms, slice and add the pan. Continue to sauté until they turn a light golden colour (about another 7 mins). Finely mince the garlic and add to the pan and cook for 1 min. Add the mince and stir-fry until the mince is browned. Remove from the heat and stir in the chopped tomatoes, tomato purée, basmati rice, herbs, salt and pepper. Make sure the mixture is well combined then fill the peppers.

Place the peppers upright in the slow cooker and pop the pepper tops back on to act as lids. Carefully add enough boiling water around the base of the peppers to cover the base to a depth of around 1.5cm (½") - probably about 80ml (1/3 cup). Put the lid on your slow cooker and cook on low for 6-8 hrs.

Cooking for 1? Prepare & Freeze Meal Tip:

Store a cooked stuffed pepper in a freezer foil tray with lid. Seal with the tray lid and freeze. To reheat, thoroughly defrost, loosen the tray lid and then bake in a preheated oven (160C fan, 350F, Gas Mark 4) for 20 mins.

Serves: 2 | Ready In: 6½ - 8 hrs | Per Serving: 195 Calories

Meals 300 Calories & Under

Slow Roast Turkey Breast with Boulangère Potatoes

Ingredients with cals per serving

- 255g (9 oz) skinless, boneless turkey breast – 128 cals
- 255g (9 oz) red potatoes – 103 cals
- 1 finger shallot (60g), finely diced – 7 cals
- 1 tbsp fresh sage leaves, chopped – 2 cals
- 1 garlic clove – 2 cals
- ½ tsp paprika – 1 cal
- ½ tsp dried Herbs de Provence – 1 cal
- ½ reduced salt chicken stock cube – 8 cal
- ½ tbsp cornflour/corn starch
- 4 sprays Frylight olive oil spray – 2 cals
- ½ tsp freshly ground black pepper
- ¼ tsp sea (kosher) salt

Directions

Mix together the paprika, Herbs de Provence, black pepper and sea salt. Spray the underside of the turkey fillet with 1 spray of Frylight olive oil spray and sprinkle over half the seasoning mix. Turn over, spritz with a further spray of olive oil spray and sprinkle over the remaining seasoning. Set aside.

Wash but don't peel the red potatoes, and slice thinly and evenly. Finely dice the shallot, garlic and fresh sage leaves. Dissolve the ½ stock cube in 240ml (1 cup) of boiling water. Spritz the bottom of the slow cooker with 2 sprays of olive oil spray. Layer over half of the potatoes slices, then scatter over the minced garlic, sage and shallots, followed by the remaining potato slices. Dissolve the cornflour/cornstarch in 2 tbsp of cold water and whisk this into the chicken stock, then pour this all over the potatoes. Lay the seasoned turkey breast on top of the potatoes. Cover the slow cooker with its lid and cook on low for 6 hrs.

Serve the cooked turkey breast on warm dinner plates with a portion of boulangère potatoes and gravy.

Serves: 2	Ready In: 6¼ hrs	Per Serving: 259 Calories

BBQ Chicken with Spicy Potato Wedges

Ingredients with cals per serving

- 410g (14½ oz) skinless, boneless chicken breast fillets – 112 cals
- 1 red onion – 8 cals
- 2 tbsp maple syrup or honey – 19 cals
- ¾ tsp each paprika, ground cumin, chipotle chile powder, divided – 6 cals
- ½ tsp dry mustard – 2 cals • 1/8 tsp ground allspice • ¼ tsp red chilli flakes
- 1 tsp fresh ginger, grated – 1 cal • 1 star anise • 2 garlic cloves, divided – 2 cals
- 400g (14oz) tinned, chopped tomatoes – 25 cals
- 1 tbsp each tomato purée, balsamic vinegar – 7 cals
- 15 oz (425g) white baking potatoes – 87 cals
- ½ reduced salt chicken stock cube – 4 cals
- 2 tsp olive oil – 22 cals
- pinch ground black pepper, sea (kosher) salt

Directions

Finely mince the garlic and peel, then finely grate the ginger root. Finely dice the red onion. If your slow cooker has a sauté function, turn it on to that setting and heat up, otherwise heat a sauté pan over a medium heat and spritz twice with Frylight spray. Add the onion and cook for 5 mins until softened, stirring occasionally. Add the minced garlic and ginger and cook for a min. Add ½ tsp each of paprika, ground cumin and chilli powder (reserving ¼ tsp each for later) along with the remaining spices and dry mustard, then cook 30 secs. Finally stir in the tomatoes, tomato purée, maple syrup/honey and balsamic vinegar and bring up to a gentle simmer. If using a sauté pan, transfer the sauce to the slow cooker. Nestle the chicken breasts into the sauce, cover the slow cooker with its lid and cook on low for 6 hrs.

Preheat the oven 200C fan, 425F, Gas Mark 7 40 mins before serving. Line a baking sheet with parchment and put into the oven to warm. Mix together the reserved ¼ tsp each of paprika, ground cumin and chilli powder. Cut the unpeeled potatoes into wedges. In a saucepan, dissolve the ½ chicken stock cube in 360 mls (1½ cups) of boiling water and bring up to the simmer. Blanch the potato wedges in the stock for 3-4 mins, then drain. Remove the baking sheet from the oven and sprinkle over the 2 tsp olive oil. Spread out the wedges on the baking tray, turning them over so that they are coated in the olive oil. Sprinkle with the spice mix. Put into the oven and cook for 15 mins. After 15 mins take out the part-cooked chips out of the oven, turn them with a spatula then return them to the oven for a further 15 mins until golden and crispy.

Serve the hot wedges with the BBQ Chicken fillets, with the sauce spooned on top.

Serves: 4 | Ready In: 6¼ hrs | Per Serving: 293 Calories

Chicken Palaver

Ingredients with cals per serving

- 250g (8¾ oz) chicken breast fillets – 68 cals
- 2 red onions (160g), diced – 16 cals
- 1 yellow bell pepper – 13 cals
- 2 garlic cloves – 2 cals
- 2 sticks celery of celery heart (80g) – 2 cals
- 1 tbsp freshly grated ginger root – 1 cal
- 14 cherry tomatoes – 8 cals
- 1 lime, zest and juice – 3 cals
- 210g (7 cups) fresh spinach – 16 cals
- 1 tsp chilli powder – 2 cals
- 2 tsp brown sugar – 10 cals
- 2 sprigs fresh thyme
- 2 tbsp crunchy peanut butter (no added salt, sugar or oil) – 43 cals
- 1 reduced salt chicken stock cube – 8 cals
- pinch sea (kosher) salt
- 1/8 tsp freshly ground black pepper
- 2 sprays Frylight olive oil spray
- 340g (1¾ cups) steamed brown basmati rice – 107 cals

Directions

The night before cooking, marinated the chicken. Finely mince the garlic with the thyme, then grate the ginger root. Put these into a non-reactive container and combine with the finely grated zest and juice of the lime, brown sugar, chilli, salt and pepper. Cube the chicken into bite-size pieces and add to the marinade. Stir well to ensure that the chicken is thoroughly coated in the marinade, seal and place in the fridge until needed. The following morning, remove the seeds and pith from the bell pepper and de-thread the celery stalk by running a vegetable peeler over the ribbed side. Dice the pepper and celery along with the red onion.

If your slow cooker has a sauté function, spritz with 2 sprays of Frylight spray. Otherwise, heat a non-stick sauté pan over a medium heat and spritz with the spray. Add the onion, pepper and celery and sauté for 7-8 mins until softened. After the onion has cooked until golden and softened, push to one side of the pan, and add the marinated chicken pieces to brown, turning so that they cook on both sides.

Whilst the chicken is browning, put the cherry tomatoes in a heat-proof bowl and pour over boiling water. Leave for 40 secs then carefully remove with a slotted spoon. When cool enough to handle, slip of the skins and discard. Dissolve the chicken stock cube in 120ml (½ cup). Returning to the sautéing chicken, when it is golden brown, add the chicken stock, then stir in the peanut butter, and whisk until dissolved. Scrap is any remnants of the marinade, then add the skinned tomatoes. If using a sauté pan, empty everything into the slow cooker. Cover the slow cooker and cook on high for 4 hrs or low for 6 hrs. When ready to serve, stir the fresh spinach into the Chicken Palaver until it has wilted. Serve in warm pasta bowls, with the hot rice.

Cooking for 1 or 2? Prepare & Freeze Meal Tip: Before stirring in the spinach, divide the Palaver into individual portions into freezer foil trays, seal and freeze. To reheat, defrost, loosen the tray lid and bake in a preheated oven (160C fan, 350F, Gas Mark 4) for 20 mins. Stir in a fresh portion of spinach and cook for a further 5 mins. Serve with rice.

Serves: 4	Ready In: 6½ - 8 hrs	Per Serving: 299 Calories

Chicken Chile Blanco

Ingredients with cals per serving

- 400g (14 oz) skinless, boneless chicken breast – 109 cals
- 236g (8½ oz) pinto beans, canned, drained and rinsed (400g/14 oz can) – 59 cals
- 25g (1½ cups) fresh coriander/cilantro – 2 cals
- 250g (2 cups) white mushrooms – 10 cals
- 150g (1½ cups) fennel, chopped – 6 cals
- 2 yellow bell peppers – 25 cals
- 1 medium white onion (80g), diced – 8 cals
- 3 green chillies (30g) – 5 cals
- 2 garlic cloves – 2 cals
- 1 lime, divided – 5 cals
- 1 tbsp cornflour/corn starch – 7 cals
- 1 reduced salt chicken stock cubes – 8 cals
- 3 dashes Tabasco
- 1 tsp cumin – 2 cals
- 1 tsp ground coriander – 2 cals
- ¼ tsp ground cayenne pepper
- ¾ tsp dried oregano – 1 cal
- 60ml (¼ cup) 0% Greek yogurt – 9 cal
- 2 sprays Frylight olive oil spray
- ½ tsp freshly ground black pepper
- ¼ tsp sea (kosher) salt

Directions

Deseed the peppers and chillies and discard the seeds. Remove the leaves from the fresh coriander (coriander) and store in the fridge until later. Finely chop the coriander stalks, chillies and garlic cloves. Dice the onion and fennel and slice the peppers. Remove and discard the skin and all visible fat from the chicken thighs.

If your slow cooker has a sauté function, turn it on to that setting and heat up, otherwise heat a sauté pan over a medium heat and spritz twice with Frylight spray. Add the peppers, onion and fennel to the pan and sauté for 5 mins until softened, stirring occasionally. Clean and slice the mushrooms and add these to the pan, cook for a further 5 mins. Add the minced coriander stalks, garlic and chillies and cook for 1 min. Stir in the dry herbs, spices, salt and pepper. If using a sauté pan, decant the cooked vegetables to your slow cooker. Dice the chicken breast and add to the slow cooker. Dissolve the stock cube in 360ml (1½ cups) of boiling water and add to the pot. Dissolve the cornflour (cornstarch) in 2 tbsp and stir into the stew. Add 3 or so dashes of Tabasco Sauce (use more or less dependent on your own taste). Give everything a really good stir, pop the lid on the slow cooker and turn the setting to low.

Cook on low for 6 hrs or on high for 4½ hrs before serving, add the rinsed and drained pinto beans and coriander leaves to the slow cooker. Squeeze in the juice of ½ lime. Give everything another good stir, pop the lid back on and cook for a further 30 mins until the beans are completely warmed through. Spoon into warm serving bowls and top each portion with a tbsp of 0% Greek yogurt, and wedges of lime from the reserved ½ lime.

Cooking for 1 or 2? Prepare & Freeze Meal Tip: Once cooked and cooled, divide individual portions seal and freeze. To reheat, defrost and then bake in a preheated oven (160C fan, 350F, Gas Mark 4) for 25 mins until piping hot.

Serves: 4 | Ready In: 4-6 hrs | Per Serving: 259 Calories

Pork & Pepper Chilli Pot

Ingredients with cals per serving

- 395g (14 oz) pork tenderloin fillet, all visible fat removed – 142 cals
- 30g pinto beans, dried – 25 cals
- 40g black (turtle) beans, dried – 19 cals
- 30g kidney beans, dried – 19 cals
- 250g (2 cups) white mushrooms – 10 cals
- 150g (1½ cups) fennel, chopped – 6 cals
- 1 yellow & 1 red bell peppers – 25 cals
- 1 medium white onion (80g), diced – 8 cals
- 3 green chillies (30g), - 5 cals
- 25g (1½ cups) fresh coriander/cilantro, - 2 cals
- 2 garlic cloves – 2 cals
- 1 lime, divided – 5 cals
- 1 tbsp corn starch/cornflour – 7 cals
- 1 reduced salt vegetable stock cube – 7 cals
- 3 dash Tabasco
- 1 tsp each ground cumin, ground coriander – 4 cals
- ¼ tsp ground cayenne pepper
- ¾ tsp dried oregano – 1 cals
- 60ml (¼ cup) 0% Greek yogurt – 9 cals
- 2 sprays Frylight olive oil spray
- ½ tsp freshly ground black pepper & ¼ tsp sea (kosher) salt

Directions

Soak the dried beans in plenty of cold water overnight (for at least 8 hours) and then rinse and put into a saucepan generously covered in cold water. Bring up to the boil and boil rapidly for 10 mins.

Deseed the peppers and chillies and discard the seeds, stalks and pith. Remove the leaves from the fresh coriander (coriander) and store in a sealed container in the fridge until later. Finely chop the coriander stalks, chillies and garlic cloves. Dice the onion and fennel and slice the peppers. Remove and discard the skin and all visible fat from the pork tenderloin and cube into bite size pieces.

If your slow cooker has a sauté function, turn it on to that setting and heat up, otherwise heat a sauté pan over a medium heat and spritz with 2 sprays of Frylight spray. Start by browning the pork pieces in batches, sautéing until golden and removing each batch to a plate whilst browning the next batch. Set aside the sautéed pork for the moment. Spritz the pan with another 2 sprays of Frylight spray and add the peppers, onion and fennel to the pan. Sauté for 5 minutes until softened, stirring occasionally. Clean and slice the mushrooms and add these to the pan, cook for a further 5 mins. Now add the minced coriander stalks, garlic and chillies and cook for 1 min. Stir in the dry herbs, spices, salt and pepper.

If using a sauté pan, decant the vegetables to your slow cooker. Drain and rinse the par-boiled beans and add these along with the sautéed pork to the slow cooker as well. Dissolve the stock cube in 480ml/ 2 cups of boiling water and add to the slow cooker. Dissolve the corn starch/cornflour in 2 tbsp and stir into the stew. Add 3 or so dashes of Tabasco Sauce (use more or less dependent on your own taste). Give everything a really good stir, pop the lid on the slow cooker and turn the setting to low. Cover with the lid and cook on low for 7 hrs.

Before serving, roughly chop the reserved coriander/cilantro leaves. Juice ½ lime, add this and half the chopped herbs to the chilli, and give everything a good stir. Then spoon into warm serving bowls and top each portion with a tbsp of 0% Greek yogurt, and wedges of lime from the reserved ½ lime and sprinkle with the chopped herbs.

Cooking for 1 or 2? Prepare & Freeze Meal Tip:

Once cooked and cooled, divide individual portions into freezer foil trays with lids. Seal with the tray lid and freeze. To reheat, thoroughly defrost and then bake in a preheated oven (160C fan, 350F, Gas Mark 4) for 25 mins until thoroughly heated.

Serves: 4 | Ready In: 7½ - 8 hrs | Per Serving: 296 Calories

Beef in Guinness Stew

Ingredients with cals per serving

- 400g (14 oz) casserole beef, trimmed of all visible fat – 143 cals
- 2 medium red onions (160g), diced – 16 cals
- 4 sticks of celery – 4 cals
- 6 medium carrots (360g) – 33 cals
- 320g (11 oz) small, new potatoes – 61 cals
- 1 tbsp cornflour (corn starch) – 7 cals
- 1 reduced salt beef stock cubes – 4 cals
- 1 330ml (1⅓ cup) bottle of Guinness or other stout beer
- ½ tsp freshly ground black pepper
- ¼ tsp sea (kosher) salt

Directions

Dice the onion and celery. Cut the carrots into 2-3 chunks. Dice the beef into large bite size pieces. Put all of these into the slow cooker (no need for any sautéing). Pour over the bottle of Guinness and crumble in the beef stock cube. Add the ground black pepper. Stir then cover with the slow cooker lid and cook on low for 5-7 hrs.

1 hr before serving, rinse the new potatoes (no need to peel) and cut into 2-3 pieces. Dissolve the cornflour/cornstarch in 2 tbsp of cold water. Stir the cornflour/cornstarch into the stew and add the potatoes, along with the salt. Give everything another good stir, pop the lid back on and cook for a further 1 hr until the potatoes are tender.

Cooking for 1 or 2? Prepare & Freeze Meal Tip:

Once cooked and cooled, divide individual portions into freezer foil trays with lids. Seal with the tray lid and freeze. To reheat, thoroughly defrost and then bake in a preheated oven (160C fan, 350F, Gas Mark 4) for 25 mins until thoroughly heated.

Serves: 4 | Ready In: 6-8 hrs | Per Serving: 298 Calories

Aromatic Duck Pilaf

Ingredients with cals per serving

- 320g (11oz) skinless duck breast fillets – 74 cals
- 1 medium red onion (80g), diced – 8 cals
- 2 medium carrots, grated (120g) – 11 cals
- 150g (2 cups) eggplant/aubergine, cubed – 6 cals
- 2 garlic cloves – 2 cals
- 3 tsp ras el hanout spice mix (or mixed spice) – 5 cals
- 1 cinnamon stick
- 2 bay leaves
- 170g (1 scant cup) brown basmati rice, dry weight – 150 cals
- 1 reduced salt chicken stock cube – 8 cals
- 2 medium tomatoes (160g), diced – 8 cals
- 4 semi-dried apricots, chopped – 13 cals
- 40ml (2 tbsp+ 2 tsp) 0% fat Greek yogurt – 6 cals
- 1 ½ tbsp flat leaf parsley, chopped – 2 cals
- 1 ½ tbsp fresh mint, chopped, divided – 3 cals
- 2 tsp flaked almonds, toasted – 5 cals
- 2 sprays Frylight olive oil spray
- ¼ tsp freshly ground black pepper
- 1/8 tsp sea (kosher) salt

Directions

In a jug, dissolve the stock cube with 360ml (1 ½ cups) of boiling water. Dice the red onion and aubergine (eggplant).

If your slow cooker has a sauté function, turn it on to that setting and heat up, otherwise heat a sauté pan over a medium heat and spritz with 2 sprays of Frylight spray. Sauté the onion and aubergine (eggplant) until softened. Remove any visible fat from the duck breast fillets and slice into think strips if not already pre-sliced. Add this to the pan and sauté until brown and caramelised.

Meanwhile, grate the carrot and finely mince the garlic clove. Add these to the pan along with the spices. Cook for a minute. Add the rice and stir thoroughly to coat the rice in the spiced mixture. If using a sauté pan, transfer the contents to your slow cooker. Dice the tomatoes and dried apricots. Add these to the slow cooker along with the chicken stock, bay leaf, cinnamon stick and a pinch each of salt and black pepper. Give everything a really good stir, and cook on low for 3-3½ hrs.

Meanwhile, heat a sauté pan over a medium heat and add the flaked almonds to toast (keep watching so that they don't burn). As soon as they are golden, remove from the pan to a piece of kitchen towel and set aside.

When ready to serve, finely chop the mint and stir ½ into the yogurt. Fork over the cooked rice to combine everything and remove the cinnamon stick. Chop the parsley and sprinkle this over the pilaf along with the toasted flaked almonds and remaining chopped mint. Serve up onto a warm plates with a spoon of minty yogurt on the side!

Serves: 4 | Ready In: 3½ - 4 hrs | Per Serving: 297 Calories

Note: Pilaf is traditionally made with lamb but substituting with skinless duck breast reduces the saturated fat by 90% whilst still retaining the rich flavour.

LEMON, THYME & PEPPER POT ROAST CHICKEN

Ingredients with cals per serving

- 2 chicken thighs, bone-in, skin removed (about 300g/10½ oz) – 137 cals
- 2 small red potatoes (160g/5½ oz) – 66 cals
- 1 medium red onion (80g/3 oz) – 16 cals
- 2 medium carrots (120g/1 cup) – 22 cals
- ½ lemon – 5 cals
- 4 sprigs of thyme
- 3 Frylight olive oil sprays – 1 cal
- ½ tsp whole peppercorns – 2 cals
- ¼ tsp sea (kosher) salt + a pinch

Directions

In a pestle and mortar, coarsely crush the peppercorns. If you don't have a pestle and mortar, don't worry, just use the end of a rolling pin to crush the corns. Cut 2 thin slices from the ½ lemon, then grate the zest from the remainder of the lemon. In a small ramekin, mix together the lemon zest, crushed peppercorns, ¼ tsp salt and the leaves pulled from 3 of the thyme sprigs.

Make sure all visible fat and skin is removed from the chicken thighs. Peel the garlic clove and cut in half. Rub the cut side over both of the chicken thighs, then spritz each thigh with 1 spray each of Frylight. Sprinkle the lemon/pepper rub evenly over the thighs and pat to make sure that the rub is well adhered to the thighs. Place 1 slice of lemon on top of each thigh.

Wash but don't peel the red potatoes, and cut in half. Trim the top from the red onion and any stringy bits from the root but leave the root in tact. Peel the onion then cut in half from top to bottom straight through the root. Cut each half into 3 wedges, again cutting through the root as this will help keep the onion wedges together during cooking. Cut each carrot into 3-4 chunks. Spritz the bottom of the slow cooker with 1 spray of Frylight. Place the onion wedges, carrots and potatoes in the bottom of the pan. Pull the leaves from the remaining sprig of thyme and scatter this over the vegetables. Juice the lemon over the vegetables and season with a pinch of sea (kosher) salt. Finally, lay the seasoned chicken breast on top of the vegetables. Cover the slow cooker with its lid and cook on low for 4-6 hrs.

Serve the pot-roasted chicken thighs on warm dinner plates with a portion of vegetables and juices from the pan.

Serves: 2	Ready In: 4 - 6 hrs	Per Serving: 251 Calories

A NOTE FROM THE AUTHOR

YOUR FEEDBACK

Thank you for choosing my Cookbook. I would love to know what you think of the recipes in this book, are any particular favourites? I would be most grateful you were able to leave a book review on the website that you purchased it from.

FURTHER TWO-DAY 5:2 DIET BOOKS

If you have enjoyed the recipes in this cookbook, you may also be interested in further books in this series:

Beginner's Guide to the Two-Day 5:2 Diet Plan & Meals For One Recipe Cookbook

The Two Day 5:2 Diet Plan Fast Diet Recipe Cookbook.

YOUR BONUS 5:2 DIET PLAN FREE GIVEAWAY

As a special Thank You to my readers, I have available an exclusive & free special bonus. Sign up for my Readers Group Newsletter and receive a FREE copy of the Two-Day 5:2 Diet Plan Fast Diet Snacks Recipe Booklet.To receive your free PDF copy of this booklet, you just need to visit http://goo.gl/SciWTU and let me know where to email it to.

LET'S STAY CONNECTED

Please do also take a look at my author blog:

MillyWhiteCooks.com

As well as details on my full range of cookbooks, you will also find articles and information on:

- Ingredients
- Cooking Techniques
- Equipment
- Health News
- Nutrition Information
- Special Offers

Every month I share a new menu of the month, showcasing recipes from my collection. You can also find me on social media too:

MillyWhiteCooks.com
facebook.com/MillyWhiteCooks
pinterest.com/MillyWhiteCooks
instagram.com/MillyWhiteCooks
twitter.com/MillyWhiteCooks
plus.google.com/+MillywhitecooksBooks/posts

Index

12508433R00038

Printed in Great Britain
by Amazon.co.uk, Ltd.,
Marston Gate.